Mitchell Symons was born in London and educated at Mill Hill School and the LSE, where he studied law. Since leaving BBC TV, where he was a researcher and then a director, he has worked as a writer, broadcaster and journalist. He was a principal writer of early editions of the board game Trivial Pursuit and has devised many television formats. He is also the author of more than thirty books, and currently writes a weekly column for the *Sunday Express*.

www.**grossbooks**.co.uk
www.**rbooks**.co.uk

How much yucky stuff do you know?

Collect all these gross facts books by Mitchell Symons!

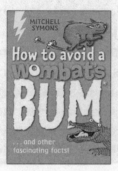

AVAILABLE NOW!

MITCHELL SYMONS

THAT'S SO GROSS!

CREEPY CRAWLIES

RED FOX

THAT'S SO GROSS! CREEPY CRAWLIES
A RED FOX BOOK 978 1 849 41188 2

Published in Great Britain by Red Fox,
an imprint of Random House Children's Books
A Random House Group Company

This edition published 2011

1 3 5 7 9 10 8 6 4 2

Set in Optima

RANDOM HOUSE CHILDREN'S BOOKS
61–63 Uxbridge Road, London W5 5SA

www.kidsatrandomhouse.co.uk
www.rbooks.co.uk

Addresses for companies within The Random House Group Limited can be found at:
www.randomhouse.co.uk/offices.htm

THE RANDOM HOUSE GROUP Limited Reg. No. 954009
A CIP catalogue record for this book is available from the British Library.

Printed in the UK by CPI Bookmarque, Croydon, CR0 4TD

*To all fans
of truly
GROSS trivia!*

INTRODUCTION

Welcome to a brand-new series of books,
which have one thing in common: they're
all intended to be ENGROSSING – with the
emphasis on the third, fourth, fifth, sixth and
seventh letters.

I've selected facts that are particularly
gruesome in the hope that you will be
disgusted and entertained in equal measure.
Occasionally – very occasionally – I have used
a fact from one of my other books (there's a list
on page two, but my editor and I know them
fondly as 'Bum', 'Bogeys', 'Poo', 'Farts', Ear Wax',
'Puke' and 'Loos'). I've only done this where it
fits in so perfectly that *not* to do it would be
even worse!

There are three other books in this series. If you
get them all, then you'll know as much as I do –
or, indeed, *more* because as soon as I discover
a new fascinating fact, I promptly forget at least
two old ones! I think my brain's storage section
has reached its full capacity.

As usual, I have a lot of thank yous. The most

important people are (in alphabetical order):
Nigel Baines, Lauren Buckland, Penny Chorlton,
Dominica Clements, Annie Eaton, Charlie
Symons and Jack Symons.

In addition, I'd also like to thank the following
people for their help, contributions and/
or support: Gilly Adams, Luigi Bonomi, Paul
Donnelley, Jonathan Fingerhut, Jenny Garrison,
Bryn Musson, Mari Roberts, Louise Symons and
Rob Woolley.

As I always write at this point, if I've missed
anyone out, then please know that – as with
any mistakes in the book – it is, as ever, entirely
down to my own stupidity.

Mitchell Symons

www.mitchellsymons.co.uk

ENGROSSING UNBELIEVABLE

Some tropical orb-weaver spiders spin webs that are so massive – over five metres across – that they can snare bats and even small birds.

In 2002 an ant colony was found on the Ishikari coast of Hokkaido in Japan that covered an area of one square mile. Inside that colony were 306 million worker ants and one million queens living in 45,000 interconnected nests. Not unreasonably, it was thought to be the biggest ant colony in existence. But, more recently, a colony measuring sixty two miles wide was found underneath Melbourne in Australia, and it's thought that there's a kind of super-colony of connected nests right across Europe that might stretch to almost 4,000 miles. Now, that really is unbelievable!

You might think that life as a termite queen is pretty good. I mean, if you *have* to be a termite, you might as well be the queen. After all, she spends most of her time laying eggs – up to 6,000 or 7,000 a day – in a nest where she's fed by worker termites, which are about a 100 times smaller than she is (though there are up to two million of them). Peel me a grape, why don't you?

But actually, life's pretty dull in the spotlight. She gets no reward for all that hard work, and as soon as she stops laying eggs, which number in the millions during her 15-year lifetime, the workers stop feeding her and she starves to death. So no retirement, no putting her feet up, no celebrity appearances on reality TV programmes (stop it, Mitch, termites *don't* appear on reality TV programmes – Ed. Yes they do: *I'm a Celebritermite . . . Get Me Out of Here!* Mitch). Nah, I've changed my mind: I think I'll become a hippo instead.

The sexton (or burying) beetle can smell a rotting corpse from over a mile away.

Aphids – also known as plant lice or greenfly – are a gardener and a farmer's enemy as they destroy plants and crops. In insect terms, however, these little creatures (they vary in length from one to 10 millimetres) are a huge success. Kill as many of them as you like and there'll always be more because they breed like crazy. An entomologist (insect expert) found that cabbage aphids had an average of 41 offspring per female, and in the six months between April and October could produce 16 generations (a generation spans from one stage in the animal's lifecycle to the same stage in the lifecycle of the offspring – usually 30 years in people). If all the descendants of one female aphid lived, there would be 1,560,000,000,000,000,000, 000,000 aphids by the end of October. That's an extraordinary number – no, not the one with all the zeros at the end of it, but the 16. What an incredible number of generations in such a short space of time. I estimate it would take a human family some 500 years to accrue as many generations as an aphid family can achieve in six months. And how many women do you know who have 41 babies – and all at the same time? In fact, so brilliant is the aphid at reproduction that females are born pregnant – just to save time! Aphids can give birth just 10 days after being born themselves.

Coming back to those 1,560,000 . . . yawn . . . 000,000 . . . nearly there . . . 000,000 . . . was it really this many? . . . 000,000 aphids. It's been estimated that if each individual aphid were packed into a snug-fitting cube, they would collectively form a tower one mile long, one mile wide, and 62,400 miles high. Yes, I too was also confused by that. Sometimes, though, I don't try to interpret stuff, I just report it and hope that brighter readers will understand. There is, of course, absolutely no law that requires an author to be cleverer than his readers . . . thank goodness!

On the subject of aphids, a group of them weighing a total of 3,500 kilos was found in an alfalfa field – this was *twice* the weight of the alfalfa hay being grown in that field.

As you probably know, insects lay eggs. Lots

of 'em. But there are a few insects – some parasitic wasps, for example – that lay a single egg containing many babies. Basically, what happens is that an egg divides into two – rather like identical twins in a human pregnancy. However, there the comparison ends, because these carry on dividing . . . and dividing . . . and dividing . . . and dividing . . . and dividing . . . and dividing . . . and dividing . . . and dividing . . . and dividing . . . resulting in as many as 2,000 young from a single egg. That's a lot of nappies . . .

The lifespan of insects, from egg to adult, usually takes a matter of a few months. As we've seen, the aphid does it a whole lot quicker, going through a whole generation in a few days. By contrast, the periodical cicada lives underground as a nymph (young form) for over 16 years. Such insects develop slowly because of environmental conditions. The wood-boring beetle is an extreme example of this phenomenon, having been known to take more than 40 years to develop in dry wood.

The fastest insect in the world is the dragonfly, which is capable of speeds up to 60 miles per hour. But that's not all! It's also fantastic at doing really complicated manoeuvres. It can hover, fly backwards, turn around in mid-air, and land instantly.

Australian termites have been known to build mounds six metres high and 30 metres wide.

Killer ants have been called the fiercest predators on Earth. They kill more creatures than all other bigger predators combined. They attack *en masse* when their mounds are disturbed, and can kill animals many times their size – even deer.

In medieval England, people used to believe that stag beetles flew around with hot coals in their jaws, setting fire to buildings. They also used to think that the stag beetle summoned thunder and lightning storms. In medieval Germany they believed this too. In fact, they associated stag beetles with Thor, the god of thunder, and thought that if they placed a stag beetle on their head, it would protect them from being struck by lightning.

278 Japanese beetles were once counted on a single apple. Glad it wasn't one that I was about to eat . . .

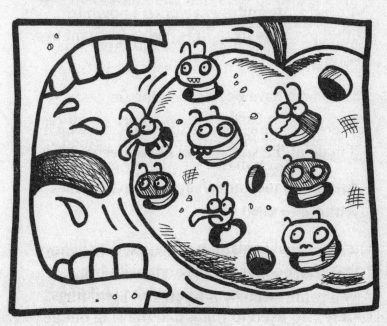

The number of insects and other arthropods (invertebrate animals with a hard outer shell and jointed legs, such as beetles, spiders or woodlice) floating and flying through the air is incredible. An American researcher named P. A. Glick collected insects in special traps that were placed on aeroplanes flying over Tallulah, Louisiana. He collected 30,033 specimens in the air, including wingless insects and spiders that were air blown. He calculated that in the air 50 – 14,000 feet above a square mile of ground there was an average of 25 million insects and other arthropods.

There are some species of insects for which a male of the species has never been found.

Tarantulas can go for up to two years without eating.

Adult cave spiders live in darkness because they can't stand the light. However, the young are strongly attracted to light. It's thought that this has evolved out of necessity to ensure the spread of the species to new areas.

If we humans had the same relative jumping ability as a flea, we would be able to achieve 215 metres in the long jump and 140 metres in the high jump.

The male lesser emperor moth is able to detect the female lesser emperor moth at a distance of up to nearly seven miles.

Spiders produce silk threads, which, thickness for thickness, have the breaking strain of iron. Spider silk is only about a 200th of a millimetre in diameter and is so light that if a spider could spin a strand around the world it would weigh less than 200 grams.

The honey bee kills more people worldwide than all the poisonous snakes combined, due to the common allergic reaction to them.

The ghost moth can whistle through its tongue.

A cockroach can survive underwater for 15 minutes.

An ant can survive underwater for two weeks.

Snails can sleep and not eat for three years.

A snail can crawl across a razor blade without getting injured because it excretes a protective slime.

Female earwigs can't distinguish their own eggs from those of other earwigs and so steal any eggs they find.

The longest insect is a walking-stick insect

that can reach a length of 55 centimetres. The eggs of walking-stick insects are among the largest in the insect world. Some eggs are more than eight millimetres long.

Hard ticks can expand from a millimetre to 30 millimetres in diameter to accommodate all the blood they feed on!

Many female creepy-crawlies are bigger than their male counterparts, but the female golden-silk orb weaver spider is five times bigger than the male. Can you imagine having a mum who was five times bigger than your dad?

Dead fleas dressed up as wedding couples were popular collectors' items back in the 1920s.

Tapeworms can live in our digestive tracts. We ingest them by eating the raw or undercooked meat of infected animals. Some tapeworms are microscopic, but they can grow to 30 metres long.

The whirligig beetle is remarkable for its divided eyes, which can see both above and below water.

Cockroaches have teeth in their stomachs.

ENGROSSING LIVES

Here's a list of how long various creepy-crawlies live for. Please be aware that this is only a rough guide: variants of the different species will live longer or shorter lives. This is especially true of beetles: those living on easily accessible and nutritionally rich 'foods' will live longer than those that don't. Note also that many of these creatures will be alive for longer in their larval stages.

Moth: less than one day (this applies to some moths and only in their final adult stages)

Mayfly: one day (or less)

Daddy-longlegs (or crane fly): two weeks

Housefly: one month

Worker bee: one month

Mosquito: three months (though the male mosquito won't live that long)

Dragonfly: four months

Spider: two years (again, the female lives longer than the male)

Pine weevil: three years

Dung beetle: four years

Black widow spider: five years (female only – the male doesn't survive mating!)

Queen bee: five years

Worker ant: five years

Stag beetle: seven years

Female ant: 15 years (her male partner will die at a much younger age – after mating)

Tarantula: 20 years (the tarantula can take 10 years just to become an adult.

Interestingly, some people keep them as pets because they can be tamed. Perhaps I should add the word 'supposedly' . . .)

African termite: up to 50 years

There are approximately 250 species of army (or killer) ants. Fortunately for us in the UK, they're mostly found in the tropical and subtropical regions of Africa, Australia and South America.

A prehistoric dragonfly that lived about 250 million years ago is the largest insect ever found. It had a full wingspan of 75 centimetres and a body-length of 45 centimetres.

Ants live in an ant colony, which consists of a series of underground chambers connected to each other and to the surface by small tunnels. Inside there are rooms designated for nurseries and food storage. The colony is built and maintained by huge numbers of worker ants, which carry tiny bits of dirt in their mandibles and deposit them near the exit of the colony where they can be used as required. All this dirt is what we call an anthill.

There are an estimated 20,000 species of ant.

There are more than 30,000 species of spider.

During the mating season, a male scorpion fly offers the female a courtship gift. This could be a dead insect or a drop of his saliva. Now that's what I call romantic!

The tropical stick bug – also known more colourfully as the walking-stick insect – can change colour in response to changes in humidity, light intensity and temperature.

Webs get dirty and torn, so lots of spiders make a new one every day. They don't waste the old one, though – they roll it up into a ball and eat it!

Houseflies use their hairy, micro-hooked, glue-oozing toe pads to walk upside down on the ceiling.

TURN UPSIDE DOWN FOR FULL EFFECT.

The world's biggest spider is the Goliath bird-eating spider (Goliath, of course, was the giant in the Bible story slain by David with his slingshot). This spider weighs 100 grams and has legs that can grow up to 25 centimetres long.

The people who name butterflies are no more original than those who name spiders, because one of the biggest butterflies is the Goliath birdwing, which lives in Indonesian rainforests and has a wingspan of up to 27 centimetres. However, it's not quite as big as the largest butterfly in the world: the Queen Alexandra's birdwing, which lives in the rain forests of Papua New Guinea and has a wingspan of up to 31 centimetres.

The giant Atlas moth of Southeast Asia, the world's biggest moth, is so huge – with a wingspan of up to 30 centimetres – that it's often mistaken for a bat when it's flying.

At five centimetres long, the Asian giant

hornet is the world's largest wasp. It flies at speeds of up to 25 miles an hour, and it attacks people.

The fairyfly is the world's smallest (known) insect. You might think from its name that it is a fly (and a cute one at that). In fact, it's a parasitic wasp that lives on the Caribbean island of Guadeloupe. This wasp is just 0.17 millimetres long and is small enough to pass through the eye of a needle. A species of featherwing beetle is probably the smallest beetle: it's just 0.25 millimetres long.

I think I've got something in my eye

There's a biting midge – also known as a punky or, even more evocatively, a no-see-um – which is the smallest fly. The largest it grows to is just six millimetres.

There's a species of termite that lives in Africa that can grow to up to 12 centimetres – making it by far the largest termite in the world.

The stag beetle is the UK's largest beetle and, indeed, is the largest terrestrial (i.e. it lives on the ground) insect in Britain. Adult females can grow up to five centimetres long and some males can reach seven centimetres. Although both can fly, the female rarely bothers to.

Believe it or not, the longest invertebrate ever recorded is also the longest creature ever recorded. In 1864 a bootlace worm measuring 55 metres was washed up on the shore of Scotland. Even at their usual length – 30 metres – bootlace worms are incredibly long, although they're rarely thicker than one centimetre.

Between them, honey bees travel a distance equal to twice around the world in order to gather enough nectar to make 400 grams of honey. When you stop to think about how hard it is to produce, it's amazing that honey is so cheap to buy!

There can be as many as 600,000 ants in a single nest.

Wasps don't have any way of storing food for the winter, which is why their colonies only last for one season. Each colony starts to break up in the autumn and the workers die of cold.

Some American states have adopted official state insects. Here are some of them:

Alabama: monarch butterfly
California: California dogface butterfly
Colorado: Colorado hairstreak butterfly

Connecticut: European praying mantis
Delaware: convergent ladybird beetle
Florida: giant swallowtail butterfly
Iowa: ladybug (ladybird)
Maryland: Baltimore checkerspot butterfly
New Mexico: tarantula hawk wasp
New York: nine-spotted ladybird
Pennsylvania: firefly
South Carolina: Carolina mantis

The reason why some states have chosen to have official insects is because they want to mark the vital role that insects play in our lives. It's for this reason that the honey bee is the most common choice of state insect, with the following states all using it: Arkansas, Georgia, Kansas, Louisiana, Maine, Missouri, Nebraska, New Jersey, North Carolina, South Dakota, Utah and Wisconsin.

ENGROSSING SURVIVAL

Praying mantises are camouflaged as protection against predators. Their body colour blends with their environment.

When surprised, a barn spider will bounce up and down in the middle of its web – probably in an attempt to look bigger and therefore more threatening.

BOING!

A wasp uses its sting for killing prey, but it can also use it very effectively to defend itself against predators. The smell from a dead wasp sends out a warning to other wasps that they are in danger and should come over fast with stings at the ready. So what form does this warning take? Is it a shout, a scream, a text message (r u free l8r?)? No, it's a pheromone, a chemical with a distinctive smell, which, when released into the air, acts as a signal to summon others.

Slugs lose water very quickly from their soft, unprotected bodies – which is why they live in damp places where they won't dry out, and also why we mostly see them after it has been raining.

Unlike its relative the snail, the slug doesn't have a hard shell so it needs protection from things that would like to eat it. That's why it secretes a sticky, slimy mucus that makes it taste absolutely disgusting.

The markings on the Atlas moth's front wing tips resemble a snake's head – making it look like a frightening target to potential predators.

Stinkbugs ooze a foul smell to protect themselves from their predators. I guess the clue's in the name.

Similarly ladybirds produce a chemical that smells and tastes so terrible that birds and other predators aren't tempted to eat them.

Fire ants have adapted to cope with flooding. When water levels in their nests rise, they form a huge ball with the workers on the outside and the queen inside. This ball then floats, and when it reaches dry land, the ants swarm out and wait for the water to go down.

When the bombardier beetle is threatened by a potential enemy, it sends out a cloud of offensive gas as a defence. This gas is created when two chemicals in its body react in the rear of its abdomen, producing an explosion, which shoots hot gas at the attacker. The beetle can aim its 'cannon' with surprising accuracy.

When the skipper caterpillar is threatened by wasps, it scatters poo in all directions. *So what,* you might think. *I would too and I'm a lot bigger than a caterpillar.* Aha, but that's to reckon without the genius of the skipper caterpillar. It doesn't poo because it's frightened, but because it knows that the wasp is more interested in its poo than it is in the caterpillar itself. In other words, it's what you might call a diversionary tactic.

The thorny devil lizard of Australia has two heads, one of which is a fake – just a knob on the back of its neck. If it's seriously threatened it will hide its real head between its front legs, which pushes the fake head on its neck forwards. Any predator will attack the fake head, instead of the real one.

Some caterpillars and other insect larvae have special glands that secrete poison when they are attacked. Predatory birds soon learn to avoid them.

When threatened, the stick insect, the weevil and the male jungle nymph will all 'play possum' – that is to say they'll fall down and pretend to be dead in the hope that their attacker will leave them alone because it wants live, not dead, prey.

The monarch butterfly is poisonous to the birds that attack it. Any bird that eats a monarch butterfly will find itself puking very soon afterwards. This might not help the poor butterfly, but it might stop that bird from attacking another one!

If it's being attacked, the wonderfully named katydid – a type of grasshopper – can shed a leg to escape.

When it comes to survival, there's nothing to touch the cockroach (not that you'd want to touch a cockroach). It's the hardiest insect and one of the oldest species on the planet. It was actually here long before the dinosaurs.

One sure-fire way to kill a cockroach (eventually) is to chop off its head – but even then it can survive for another nine days. That is one tough insect!

Some species of cockroach are capable of remaining alive for a month without food and are able to survive on almost anything (like the glue on the back of postage stamps). Some can go without air for nearly an hour by slowing down their heart rate. In one experiment, cockroaches were able to recover from being submerged underwater for half an hour. Even after they die they carry on breaking wind, releasing methane for another 18 hours.

People always say that if there were a nuclear war the cockroach would be the only animal to survive. It's not a bad guess as the cockroach is at least five times more resilient than we are and has a much higher tolerance – perhaps 10 times as much – to the radiation that would come from nuclear bombs than any mammal. Interestingly, though, the fruit fly has an even greater tolerance of radiation – so maybe they'd make it through a nuclear holocaust too.

The soft body of the potato beetle larva is extremely appealing to birds and other predators. So it makes itself a little less appealing by covering itself in its own poisonous poo. A shield that's as good as a shell any day!

ENGROSSING DAMAGE

Every year, insects eat about a third of our planet's total food crop. To put it a different way, the food we lose would more than feed all the world's poor and starving people with plenty left over to put in a gigantic freezer in the Antarctic (in case of a bad harvest).

Take the western corn rootworm – or, rather, don't (especially if you're an American corn producer). These are beetle larvae that can destroy huge amounts of corn if left untreated. In the USA, it is estimated that 50,000 square miles of the 125,000 square miles of corn fields are infested with corn rootworms, and that area is expected to grow over the next 20 years. The US Department of Agriculture estimates that corn rootworms cost $1 billion (£625 million) in lost revenue each year – made up of $800 million (£500 million) in lost corn and $200 million (£125 million) for the cost of pesticides to get rid of the rootworms.

That's just one species of insect (remember there are more than a million named ones and anything from six to 20 million unnamed ones, although not all insect species are pests) – and one specific crop. The alarming fact is that *every* crop has its own insect predator.

For example, the coconut hispine beetle feeds on young leaves and damages coconut palm trees (both the seedlings and the mature trees), causing a dramatic decrease in the coconut yield of the trees. Here's an example of just how devastating an insect you'd never even heard of can be. The coconut industry in the Philippines is worth some £500 million a year. That's a lot of money for one of the poorest countries in the world. In 2007 the Philippine government was forced to quarantine – that's to say seal off – the capital and 26 provinces because they had become infested with the coconut hispine beetle.

You might well have heard of the Colorado potato beetle because it is such a terrible pest. As its name suggests, it feeds on potato plants – destroying whole crops. It can only be killed by using expensive pesticides, but it has now developed resistance to

all major insecticides. Fortunately, in the UK the Colorado beetle only comes in on imported farm produce, but it is potentially so serious a pest that it must be reported to the government if it's spotted. By the way, the Colorado beetle also attacks other plants – like tomatoes and aubergines.

These beetles are a huge problem – you might even say 'bugbear' – for commercial farmers in the West, but there's another creature that is an even bigger threat to farmers in the poorer parts of the world: the locust. In fact, to be really specific, the desert locust, which has threatened agricultural production in Africa and Asia for hundreds of years. In any given year, the livelihoods of at least 1/10th of the people in the world are damaged by this insect.

Here's how desert locusts operate. The clue's in the name: they live in the desert where there's rarely any rain. When it does rain, plants that have been lying dormant start sprouting very quickly, but the locusts also quickly increase in numbers. All too soon, the drought returns so the (by now) very hungry locusts all get together in one huge gang, fighting over what little greenery remains. That's why the desert locust is the most dangerous of all the locusts because of the ability of swarms to fly rapidly across great distances, moving from place to place and destroying all the vegetation in their wake.

In the past, people didn't understand this and therefore assumed that they were a plague sent by God. Indeed, a plague of locusts is specifically mentioned in the Bible (when Moses was trying to flee the pharaoh of Egypt).

In 2004 a swarm of desert locusts flew across West and North Africa. They did damage in excess of £125 million.

It isn't just crops that are destroyed by insects. Trees are also vulnerable. In fact, more trees are lost to insects each year than are destroyed by forest fires.

The bark beetle is an example. It is a terrible pest because it carries Dutch elm disease from infected breeding sites to healthy elm trees. The spread of this disease by the beetle has led to the devastation of elm trees in many parts of Europe and North America.

The mountain pine beetle does untold damage to pine trees. Under the right – or, rather, *wrong* – circumstances it is the single most destructive insect pest of mature pine forests. The recent infestation in British Columbia is the largest ever experienced in Canada.

Meanwhile, termites do more damage in the USA every year than all the fires, storms and earthquakes combined. A termite colony will usually contain 200,000 to 2,000,000 workers – although it may house more than three million individuals. Termites chew wood, and their favourite nesting area is inside houses, where they eat and eat until there's nothing left. It is estimated that Americans spend more than £60,000,000 in repairs to termite damage every year.

The death watch beetle attacks older wooden buildings in the UK. It's particularly keen on hard woods such as oak and chestnut – especially where there's been some fungal decay, but it's reckoned that the pest actually enters the buildings it infests at the time they're built.

The boll weevil has cost cotton producers in the USA billions of dollars since it first entered that country from Mexico in the late 19th-century.

ENGROSSING INSECT NAMES

It's reckoned that there are some six to 20 million species of insect on the planet at the present time, and most have never been given names – scientific or common. It's very difficult to estimate the numbers of species that have yet to be discovered and named.

No more than a million species currently have scientific names. Given that taxonomists (specialists who name and classify living things) around the world describe and name about 10,000 insect species a year, at the lowest estimate it would take at least 600 years before every species on earth was named. Of course, by the end of that time, many species would have become extinct. Of all the million species that *have* been named – one third (about 350,000) are beetles, or Coleoptera. They're followed by the Lepidoptera (butterflies and moths), with 165,000 different species; true flies, or Diptera, with about 120,000 species; and then Hymenoptera (wasps and bees), with 103,000 species. These four orders make up more than 80 per cent of all named insect species.

Here are some wonderfully named beetles:

Bacon beetle, black spruce longhorn beetle, blister beetle, bloody-nosed beetle, blue soldier beetle, brassy willow beetle, carpet beetle, cobweb beetle, dead-nettle leaf beetle, depressed flour beetle, devil's coach-horse, devil's-bit jewel beetle, dung beetle, flamboyant flower beetle, golden-haired longhorn beetle, green tiger beetle, green tortoise beetle, hairy click beetle, hairy fungus beetle, harlequin beetle, Hercules beetle, lily beetle, lunar-spotted mimic-beetle, mealy bug destroyer lady beetle, Mexican bean beetle, mustard beetle, pygmy beetle, rainbow leaf beetle, raspberry beetle, rhinoceros beetle, rustic sailor beetle, screech beetle, sexton beetle, short-circuit beetle, skullcap leaf beetle, soldier beetle, stag beetle, strawberry seed beetle, striped flea beetle, sulphur beetle, turnip mud beetle, wasp beetle, western blood-red lady beetle, whirligig beetle, yellow-shouldered ladybird.

Here are some of the stories behind these extraordinary names:

The dung beetle gets its name from its favourite choice of food. That's why it's not called the baked-beans-on-toast beetle or the cheese-string beetle. Dung beetles *love* dung in the same way that I *love* chocolate raisins and chocolate peanuts (ideally mixed). Both the adult dung beetles and their larvae eat their own bodyweight in dung every day. Perhaps one day I'll eat my own bodyweight in chocolate raisins and chocolate peanuts. When my friends read

THE BAKED BEANS ON TOAST BEETLE

this, more than one will say, 'But Mitch, surely you already have . . .'

The rhinoceros beetle gets its name from the pointed projection on the front of its head, makes it look a little like a (very small) rhinoceros. Actually, only the male rhinoceros beetle has this pointed thingy; the female rhinoceros beetle just has a small bump.

The wasp beetle gets its name because of its ability to do a superb impression of a common wasp. This is a fascinating example of a harmless insect imitating a more dangerous one in order to protect itself.

The short-circuit beetle gets its name from the way it chews through lead-shielded cables. Moisture then enters the cables and causes short circuits.

Do you know who or what a sexton is? It's a church officer charged with the maintenance of the church buildings and the surrounding graveyard. So if I tell you that the sexton (or burying) beetle digs a hole beneath a dead animal and then pulls the body down into the hole, you'll understand how it got its name.

Regular readers – and bless you all – will be familiar with the concept of a *syllogism*. Put simply, it's where you take information and make an incorrect deduction. For example, all humans have legs. Agreed? All dogs have legs. Yes, that's also true. So does that mean that all humans are dogs? Of course it doesn't! Well, that's a syllogism (and it's *definitely* worth sharing with your English teacher if you want to impress them).

I mention all this because I'm keen for you to avoid making one when I tell you about burying beetles. A sexton beetle is a burying beetle, but that doesn't mean that all burying beetles are sexton beetles. Do you see what I mean? Anyway, the burying beetle gets its name because it buries the remains of small vertebrates – like birds and rodents – for its larvae to eat.

The devil's coach-horse is a species of rove beetle (of which we have around 1,000 different species in Britain alone). Rove beetles get their name because they're always on the move (or, indeed, *roving*). The devil's coach-horse is a fast-moving beetle that is capable of flying – but rarely does. It is an unusual-looking beetle as its wing covers are very short, exposing its segmented abdomen, which it can curl over its back a bit like a scorpion's tail. It gets its name partly from its speed, but also from mythology, where it was considered a symbol of corruption (and therefore an emissary of the devil). Its other names include devil's footman, devil's coachman and devil's steed. People believed it had the power to kill on sight, and that it would eat sinners. When the beetle raised its tail, it was thought to be casting a curse. In fact, it wasn't a curse, but something far worse: a truly foul smell from its bottom! It can also squirt a stinking brown fluid from its mouth and bottom, so you can see why people thought it was cursed!

The bloody-nosed beetle gets its common name from its habit of releasing a bright red fluid from its mouth when it feels at all threatened. It's also known as the blood spewer or blood-spewing beetle. Bet it doesn't get many party invitations!

The carpet beetle feeds on – yes, you've guessed it – carpets. It also damages furniture and clothing, and is a serious household pest.

Did you know that there are more than 1,000 different species of stag beetle? Well, you do now. They're called stag beetles because the large and distinctive mandibles on the male's head are thought to resemble a deer's antlers. Despite their gruesome appearance, these antlers aren't used for biting, but to fight other males for the best breeding sites. Funnily enough, the much smaller antlers of the female *are* used for biting, and can inflict a sharp nip.

The whirligig beetle is a water beetle that normally lives on the surface of the water. It gets its name because when it's alarmed, it swims rapidly in circles – like a whirligig: an object that spins.

The blister beetle gets its name from the fact that it secretes a poison that makes very painful blisters on the skin of anyone unlucky enough to attract its attention.

Here are some wonderfully named spiders:

Bark crab spider, Brazilian salmon tarantula, Brazilian white-knee tarantula, burrowing wolf spider, California trapdoor spider, Chilean rose tarantula, cinnamon tarantula, crab spider, curlyhair tarantula, dewdrop spider, garden ghost spider, Goliath bird-eating spider, government canyon bat cave meshweaver, greater horned tarantula, hammock spider, king baboon tarantula, Mexican bloodleg tarantula, Mexican orange beauty tarantula, pirate wolf spider, robber baron cave meshweaver, spiny-backed orbweaver, star-bellied orbweaver, striped-knee tarantula, thinlegged wolf spider, Togo starburst tarantula, trashline orbweaver, turret spider.

Here are some of the stories behind these extraordinary names:

The Goliath bird-eating spider (also called the Goliath bird-eater) was named by

19th-century explorers who witnessed one eating a hummingbird.

Crab spiders get their name because they resemble crabs, with two front pairs of legs angled outwards and bodies that are flattened and often angular. Also, like crabs, they can move backwards and sideways.

The striped-knee tarantula – also known as the Costa Rican zebra tarantula – is so called because it is black with white stripes near the joints of its legs.

The skeleton tarantula gets its name from the skeleton-like markings on its legs, making it look remarkably like the spider version of a Hallowe'en black-and-white skeleton costume.

After reading up on these spiders and their names, something emerges really rather quickly. The people who discover and name spiders are a very literal bunch of people. Something has black-and-white stripes? Then it's a zebra spider. It lives in a cave? Where? Europe, you say? OK, let's call it the European cave spider. And that's why I love spider names – because I enjoy conjuring up an image of the spiders from them.

Here are some wonderfully named butterflies:

Black-veined white, dark-green fritillary, dingy skipper, green hairstreak, green-veined white, grizzled skipper, lime swallowtail, little blue marbled white, marsh fritillary, orange-barred sulphur, rare tiger helicon.

Here are some wonderfully named crickets and grasshoppers:

Bog bush-cricket, dark bush-cricket, field

cricket, great green bush-cricket, lesser
marsh grasshopper, long-winged conehead,
meadow grasshopper, speckled bush-
cricket.

**Here are some wonderfully named
dragonflies:**

Black darter, black-tailed skimmer,
demoiselle agrion, emerald damselfly,
four-spotted darter, golden-ringed hawker,
keeled skimmer, southern hawker, white-
legged damselfly.

Here are some wonderfully named flies:

Bee fly, bluebottle, drone fly, greenbottle,
hornet fly, horsefly, hoverfly, robber fly,
stiletto fly, stilt-legged fly.

Here are some wonderfully named moths:

Angle shades moth, bagworm moth, bright-
line brown-eye moth, broom moth, buff
ermine moth, cabbage moth, common

footman moth, cream-spot tiger moth,
death's head hawk moth, elephant hawk
moth, garden tiger moth, goat moth,
gold spot moth, grass emerald moth,
hummingbird hawk moth, jersey tiger moth,
old lady moth, orchard swallowtail moth,
rosy rustic moth, ruby tiger moth, scalloped
oak moth, snout moth, spinach moth,
vampire moth, willow beauty moth.

The vampire moth of Australia feeds on, you guessed it – blood.

The praying mantis gets its name because of its posture. It holds its front legs together as if it were praying.

The fire ant is so-called because if it bites people, it leaves a nasty burn and they feel like their skin is on fire.

Dracula ants are so-called because they suck the blood of their young.

The assassin bug really earns its name. It

waits until a bedbug has filled itself up with someone's blood and then attacks the bedbug and sucks out the newly consumed blood from its stomach.

The larva of the ant lion is often called a 'doodlebug'. The odd winding, spiralling trails it leaves look like someone has doodled in the sand.

Because of its short lifespan, the mayfly is also called the 'one-day fly' or the 'dayfly'.

A male driver ant is sometimes called a sausage fly because its bloated stomach looks like a sausage.

The name 'earwig' comes from the mistaken belief (or 'old wives' tale') that earwigs burrow into people's brains through their ears and then lay their eggs.

ENGROSSING STRENGTH

The strongest insect is the rhinoceros beetle, which is so powerful it can carry 850 times its own weight – which would be like you trying to carry a jumbo jet on your back. Don't try this at home – always assuming that you keep a jumbo jet in your back garden . . .

Dung beetles can move mountains of manure that are 100 times heavier than them.

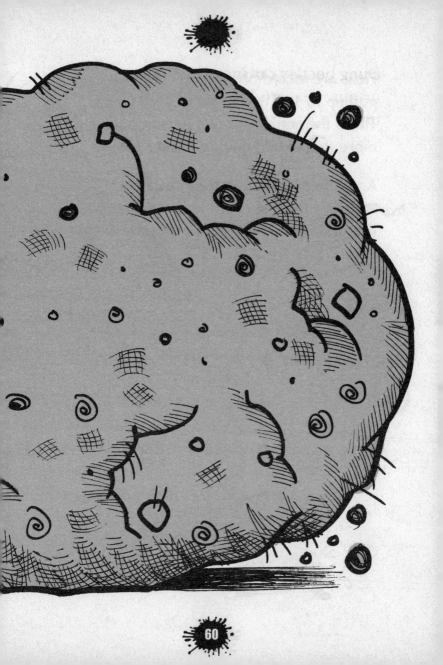

Fleas are incredibly strong – one flea can pull up to 160,000 times its own weight. That's the equivalent of a person pulling more than 2,000 double-decker buses!

Ants can lift 20 times their own body weight. I can't even lift *half* of mine (but then I do have rather a lot of body weight).

ENGROSSING - INTERESTING

80 per cent of the creatures on Earth have six legs.

All spiders spin silk, but not all make webs.

When it gets hot, some dragonflies point their long abdomens right at the sun. This way the sun's rays only hit the tip of the abdomen and not the whole length, keeping the dragonfly much cooler.

People wear amber as jewellery, but what they're actually doing is carrying around extremely old insects! For those pretty orange amber stones sometimes contain insects, which have been fossilized in perfect shape for 35 – 90 million years.

Fleas can live for up to 100 days without food.

All spiders have venomous fangs, but not all of them are able to pierce human skin.

According to researchers, the favourite colour of flies is red, followed by orange, black, violet, green, blue, white and yellow.

When ants find food, they lay down a chemical trail using pheromones, so that other ants can find their way from the nest to the food source.

The loudest insect in the world is the male cicada. He can be heard from over 400 metres away.

Some South Pacific island people use fishing nets made from spiders' webs spun between bamboo shoots.

The firefly – or lightning bug as it's also known – produces its light from a chemical substance called luciferin. When this is mixed with oxygen, a chemical reaction takes place that produces light.

The shiny wing covers of metallic wood-boring beetles were used by the ancient Incas to make ceremonial costumes.

A flea can jump over 150 times its own height and it can do this – up to the height of a metre – 30,000 times without a break. When they jump, fleas accelerate 50 times faster than the space shuttle, and they can jump in any direction. If only we could do that!

In late summer and early autumn –
particularly if the weather's hot and a storm
is threatening – you might see swarms of
flying ants. These swarms are nothing less
than a multiple 'ant wedding' in which male
and female ants take to the air in order
to mate. After mating the males die. The
females go off to set up new colonies and
shed their wings.

Mexican jumping beans jump because of a
moth larva inside the bean moving around.

The red admiral butterfly can locate sugar in liquids that are 200 times more dilute than the human tongue can taste. In other words, its ability to taste sugar is 200 times sharper than ours!

Cockroaches are among the biggest contributors to global warming, since they break wind every 15 minutes.

Insect flatulence may account for one-fifth of all the methane put out by our planet.

Termites are also prodigious farters; indeed, dogs trained to sniff out termites are actually following their farts.

Honey bees air-condition their hive when it gets hot – some of the workers position themselves at the entrance and fan their wings. When it gets really hot, they bring droplets of watered-down honey with them, which cools the air even more.

No two spider webs are exactly the same. A

bit like human fingerprints, I guess.

Some cockroaches are so fast they can run 50 times their own body length per second.

The fire ant, which is about the size of a rice grain, has a sting more painful than that of a hornet.

Sometimes different species of insects get together in what might be called a symbiotic relationship (loosely translated as

'You scratch my back and I'll scratch yours!') Some species of ant, for instance, defend aphids from predators, building shelters for them, and even taking them into their nest during bad weather. In return the aphids provide the ants with honeydew – a sweet, sticky secretion they make from plant sap that the ants like to eat.

Why do bees hum? No, this isn't a Christmas-cracker joke, so the answer's not 'Because they don't know the words.' They make that sound because their wings are beating at a rate greater than 10,000 times a minute.

The heaviest cockroach is the Australian giant burrowing cockroach, which can reach eight centimetres in length and weigh more than 30 grams. The longest cockroach is the giant cockroach of Central and South America which grows to 9 centimetres long.

As well as for web-building and prey-catching, spiders also use their silk to make parachutes as a means of transport.

Elsewhere in this book, I've told you about female black widow spiders, which kill their male partners after mating. Now let me introduce you to the female nursery web spider, which sometimes also attempts to eat the male after mating. To reduce the risk of this, the male will often present the female with a gift – something like a fly – in the hope that this will satisfy her hunger so that she doesn't kill him.

ENGROSSING FEEDING HABITS

The African giant cricket eats human hair.

Every day, a female flea consumes 15 times her own body-weight in something (or someone) else's blood.

Leeches can drink up to five times their weight in blood.

The larvae of death-watch beetles eat wood, including building timbers, causing considerable damage.

The praying mantis eats its prey upside down, holding its victims in its spiny forelegs so that it doesn't drop them.

A snail will sometimes eat another snail by drilling a hole in its victim's shell.

Wasps eat each other as well as bits of other insects.

All spiders are carnivorous – that's to say meat-eating. They're also cannibals, and will eat other spiders. Some hunt by day, others at night, and some do both.

Spiders can't eat solid food so they have to liquefy their prey before consuming it. They do this by pouring their digestive juices on their prey. This softens it up to the point where it becomes a sort of soup, which the spider sucks up. However, it's a very time-consuming operation. Let's say the spider has captured a large fly. It can take several hours before it's liquid enough for the spider to consume. Add in the time it takes to 'drink' and it can last for 12 hours in total.

Hey, waiter, there's no fly in my soup!

Dung beetles feed on fresh animal poo, which they gather into balls, rolling them with their hind legs, and then bury. It sounds disgusting – and it is – but it's also terribly useful as they get rid of so much of the poo that animals drop. In fact, Australia imported 45 different species of dung beetle from various parts of the world to help reduce its mountains of cow dung. In Texas, it's estimated that dung beetles consume 80 per cent of all cattle dung.

In Africa, a researcher decided to keep
watch on a 1.5 kilo pile of elephant poo
(don't knock it: it's a job that someone has
to do). Anyway, he observed that the pile of
poo attracted 16,000 dung beetles of various
shapes and sizes, which between them ate
and/or buried the poo completely in just
two hours.

You'll note that I wrote 'buried': dung
beetles love burying dung – it's their
equivalent of a day out at Alton Towers. A
typical dung beetle can bury 250 times its
own weight in a night.

Female water spiders build underwater 'diving bell' webs, which they fill with air and use for digesting prey.

Female scorpions sometimes eat their own offspring.

If it's not disturbed, a horsefly will suck blood from its victim for over half an hour.

Soldier termites can't feed themselves and so they must be fed by the workers.

Honeypot ants act like a supermarket home delivery system. Their bloated stomachs contain nectar which they collect then bring back to the nest to feed to other members of the colony. This is how it works. The worker honeypot ants return from gathering nectar and regurgitate it for other ants, which, in turn, become 'larder' ants, storing it for when food is scarce in the colony – when they'll regurgitate this already regurgitated food for the other ants to eat. If this sounds extraordinary, then I should explain that honeypot ants have two stomachs. One stomach holds the food for itself; the second stomach is for food to be shared with other honeypot ants.

Slugs eat decaying plant matter and the bits of plants that we humans don't eat. They have tentacles through which they can smell food from a distance of several metres.

The tarantula is a nocturnal creature – that's to say it comes out at night to find its food. It's large enough to eat the animals that smaller spiders simply can't catch, including toads, frogs, small birds and even snakes and lizards.

ENGROSSING BODY PARTS

All insects have three body parts – a head, a thorax (middle) and an abdomen. They also have six (jointed) legs, which are always attached to the thorax, not the abdomen, and two antennae, which they use as sensors.

Spiders are definitely creepy-crawlies, but they're NOT insects – they're arachnids, a group that includes spiders, harvestmen and mites. A spider's body is divided into two parts – a combined head and thorax (cephalothorax) and a large abdomen – and has eight legs (four pairs) attached to the cephalothorax. Most spiders have eight eyes, arranged in two rows of four. Unlike insects, arachnids don't have antennae or wings.

Mosquitoes have 47 teeth.

Flies' eyes don't have any eyelids so they rub their eyes with their feet to keep them clean.

The neck of the male long-necked weevil is twice the length of its body.

A caterpillar has more than 2,000 muscles.

The Tanzanian parasitic wasp is smaller than the eye of a housefly.

Ants don't have lungs. So how do they survive? Well, they have tiny holes all over their bodies called spiracles, which take in oxygen and expel carbon dioxide.

The housefly – like all flies – has compound eyes, each of which has more than 4,000 lenses.

The click beetle has a special hinge on its thorax. By arching its body, it can create a tension on the hinge, like a coiled spring. This can be suddenly released, causing the beetle to leap into the air at a speed of more than two metres per second. It's name comes from the 'click' sound it makes when this happens.

There's a species of cicada with pores (tiny holes) in the side of its thorax that let water in and out. This acts like sweat and helps to cool the insect down.

Another thing to know about the cicada – which is also known as the jar fly or the dry fly because of the dry shell that it sheds – is that it has its ears (or, to be more accurate, 'hearing organs') in its stomach. By the way, although cicadas do a lot of damage to crops, they pose no threat whatsoever to humans. We, on the other hand, pose a huge threat to them – particularly in Malaysia and China, where they're eaten (especially the females, which are meatier) and their shells used in medicine.

Crickets have their 'hearing organs' in their knees – in an oval slit on their forelegs.

PARDON ?

The creature with the largest brain (relative to its body) is . . . bet you can't guess it . . . the ant!

The flatworm – which can be found near water – can be cut into two or even three parts, and each bit will grow a new head and/or tail.

Stag beetles have stronger mandibles (jaws) than humans – relative to size.

If a cockroach breaks a leg, it can grow another one.

ENGROSSING
INSECT-EATING

It's not only animals, birds and other insects that feed on insects . . . human beings from all over the world do so too. I've brought you some of these strange dishes in previous books, but it seems like an appropriate time to remind you.

I don't think I'm going to like this chapter

Here are some gross insect dishes from around the world:

Wasp pupae (Japan)

Cooked tarantulas (Cambodia – provided the highly irritant hairs, the spiders' main defence system, are removed first)

Silkworm omelette (China)

Crisp roasted termites (Swaziland)

Weaver moths and their nests (Democratic Republic of Congo)

Polynesian seaworms (Samoa)

Bee grubs in coconut cream (Thailand)

Queen white ants (South Africa)

Large Pandora moth caterpillars (Paiute People of Oregon)

Silkworm pupae soup (Vietnam)

White ant pie (Tanzania)

Banana worm bread (Iowa State University, USA)

Earthworm broth (China)

Red ant chutney (India)

Roasted palmworms with orange juice (West Indies)

Broiled beetle grubs (Japan)

Fried cactus caterpillars (Mexico)

Locust dumplings (North Africa)

Sun-dried maggots (China)

Roasted caterpillars (Laos)

Boiled locusts (Vietnam)

If, like me, you're British, then don't go feeling too superior about the dietary habits of our foreign friends. People eat insects in this country too – only here we don't have the excuse (as people from some of the countries above do) that we can't afford anything else. I have been to restaurants that 'boast' all sorts of ghastly creepy-crawlies, to be told by the waiters that they do actually have people eating them – and not just (as you'd have thought) for a bet.

While we're on the subject, let's not forget our neighbours: the average French citizen eats 500 snails a year.

And then there's *I'm A Celebrity . . . Get*

Me Out of Here! Now here I must make a confession: this programme is a guilty pleasure of mine, but I still find it hard to watch people – even Katie Price (or Jordan, depending on her mood) – eating insects, especially live ones (the insects not the people).

The other reason why people in countries that don't have a tradition of eating insects might do just that is if they're trying to break records. Here are six:

- 100 live maggots in five minutes, 29 seconds

- 144 snails in 11 minutes, 30 seconds

- 12 slugs in 12 minutes

- 94 worms in 30 seconds

- 36 cockroaches in one minute

- 60 earthworms in three minutes, six seconds.

ENGROSSING HUNTERS

The praying mantis is carnivorous and feeds on insects. It can also attack small reptiles and birds. If there's no other food available, it will turn on its own and eat other praying mantises.

The assassin bug kills its prey by injecting its deadly venom and then sucks up the liquefied dissolving prey as a meal. The assassin bug's saliva is so poisonous that it can temporarily blind humans.

Unlike other spiders, the crab spider doesn't build webs to trap its prey. Instead, it hunts by ambush. Its amazing camouflage makes it look like a flower or a leaf, and it will sit camouflaged in vegetation and wait for visiting insects. Then it pounces.

The female bolas spider eats moths, but

catches them in an unusual way: it fishes for them! It uses a strand of silk with a globule of a sticky substance at the end, which smells similar to the pheromone that moths use to attract mates. The spider swings its 'line' at its moth prey until it catches one.

Some old-world tarantulas rub special hairs off their abdomen and flick them at their attackers. These can cause an allergic reaction or, if inhaled, can be fatal to the attacker.

whoops... think I flicked too hard

The Goliath bird-eating spider of South America – a massive arachnid that's the size of a large plate – eats, despite its name, mainly insects, small rodents and frogs, although it is certainly large enough to eat birds, and will take nestlings. It hunts its prey in a simple but effective way – by sneaking up to it and sinking its fangs in. The venom from the fangs paralyses the prey, enabling the spider to liquefy it while it's still alive and then, as we've seen earlier, 'drink' it up.

Many plants depend on insects to pollinate them. To attract these insects to their flowers to feed on their nectar they use ultraviolet patterns. Clever spiders use silk that reflects ultraviolet light, thereby attracting insects and fooling them into thinking they are seeing lovely harmless flowers.

As we've seen, different types of spider have different ways of capturing their victims: most jump on them or use their webs to snare them. However, all spiders have extremely sensory hairs on their bodies and legs, and they can detect the slightest change in air currents about them, which might indicate the movement of prey. They also have lightning-fast reactions, and a sense of smell that enables them to hunt by scent sometimes better than they can by sight.

ENGROSSING KILLERS

The female black widow spider can kill as many as 20 mates in a single day. It was Rudyard Kipling, the man who brought us *The Jungle Book*, who wrote that 'the female of the species is deadlier than the male'. And to think he never met a female black widow spider . . .

While we're on the subject . . . the venom of a female black widow spider is more potent than that of a rattlesnake. Best keep away from both of 'em, I say.

Soldier termites squirt a substance at both their prey and at their enemies, which first paralyses them and then chokes them to death.

Sanguinary ants raid the nests of other ant tribes, kill the queen and kidnap the workers.

If an insect intrudes into a beehive, honey bees can completely surround it, while vibrating their bodies together. The heat this creates literally cooks the insect intruder to death.

When a queen bee lays the eggs that will develop into new queens, only one will actually survive. The first new queen that emerges destroys all the other queens while they're still in their cells and then reigns alone. This is the only time queen bees ever sting.

An insect's worst enemies are other insects: of the millions of insects that are carnivorous, most feed on other insects.

ENGROSSING ONLYS

The honey bee is the only insect that produces food eaten by humans. It's also the only insect that can be moved for the express purpose of pollination, and the only insect to leave its sting behind when it attacks (thus causing its own death).

The praying mantis is the only insect that can turn its head 360 degrees. It's also the only creature on Earth with just one ear.

The diving-bell spider is the only spider that spends its whole life under water. However, it still breathes air, which it traps in a bubble held by hairs on its abdomen and legs.

The moose fly is the only insect known to attack in combat formation.

The Xerxes butterfly is the only insect with a common (as opposed to Latin or scientific) name that begins with an 'x'.

The flightless midge is the only true free-living insect that lives in the sub-zero temperatures of the Antarctic.

ENGROSSING CREEPY-CRAWLIES AND US

There are a lot of creepy-crawlies on Earth. For starters, 95 per cent of all the creatures on the Earth are insects. It's reckoned that there are approximately 10 quintillion (10,000,000,000,000,000,000) individual insects alive on our planet right now. Go on, start counting!

The total weight of insects in the world is three times the weight of all other living creatures.

There are some 200 million insects for every person in the world. There are one million ants for every person in the world.

The world's termites outweigh the world's humans by 10 to one.

All the earthworms in America weigh 55 times what all the people weigh.

The weight of insects eaten by spiders every year is greater than the total weight of the entire human population.

With over 300,000 different species, one out of every four creatures on Earth is a beetle.

Every year, insects consume 10 per cent of the world's food supply.

There are more insects in one square mile of rural land than there are human beings on the entire Earth.

Every time you step outside you walk upon thousands of insects. In an oak forest in Pennsylvania, researchers counted the number of arthropods – that's insects, arachnids and crustaceans, or creepy-crawlies to you and me – in leaf litter and soil from a sample that was just 30 centimetres square and 7.5 centimetres deep.

How many creepy-crawlies do you think

they found in that tiny sample? The answer was 9,759.

Britain has more than 600 species of spiders – fortunately, all of them harmless to us. Other places are not so lucky. Here are just two of the most dangerous spiders in the world – both found in Australia. The bite of the male funnel-web spider can kill a person in 15 minutes. With the redback spider, it's the bite of the female that can kill. With both these spiders, there have been no human deaths since the antivenom was developed.

Houseflies are a terrible menace to us and to our health as they spend their time in poo (animal and human), dead creatures and rubbish, where they pick up bacteria and viruses. They can carry more than 100 diseases, including typhoid, cholera, dysentery and tuberculosis, as well as parasitic worms, all of which they then proceed to share with us by walking all over our food and pouring saliva onto it.

Adult flies usually live for up to a month. They have the potential to devastate mankind: it's been calculated that one pair of flies could produce over 100,000,000,000,000,000,000 flies in their lifetime. But for that to happen, each generation would have to live, and that's where (our chums in this instance) the spiders come in. Those arachnids that we've all learned to hate and, in some cases, fear are the most important bulwarks between us and the wretched flies as they prey on them voraciously. So think about that the next time you're trying to drown a spider in the bath (and why is it so difficult to get them to go down the plughole: anyone would think they didn't want to . . .). Even so, flies are still a problem for mankind. After studying 300,000 flies, researchers concluded that the average fly carries two million bacteria on its body.

Bear in mind that houseflies can't bite or chew, so if they want to consume anything at all solid – even dried blood – they have to suck it up. The way they do this is particularly gross: first they scrub the substance with the bristles on the end of their proboscis. This frees up food particles, if they're not already loose and crumbly. Then it pours saliva and digestive juices onto its meal. These break down the food so they can then suck everything up like some sort of ghastly vacuum cleaner.

It's because of where houseflies have been and how they conduct themselves that you must always keep them away from food. If they do land on it, you have to wash it if you possibly can before eating it yourself.

The best thing to do is kill them (unless you're a Buddhist who doesn't believe in taking any life – including insects'), but bear in mind that it's extremely hard to swat a housefly as their reactions are some 12 times faster than ours.

It's important not to confuse flies with fleas. They're NOT interchangeable. Flies are so called because they, er, fly. This distinguishes them from fleas, which don't because they don't have any wings. The flea, however, is an expert at piercing skin and sucking blood and, in doing so, can transmit terrible diseases.

Fleas are blood-sucking creatures that live on humans and animals – including household pets. They thrive in carpets and in soft squidgy sofas and armchairs.

How fleas find their hosts – or targets, as they might more accurately be described – is gruesome, but fascinating. The female flea lays eggs that turn into grub-like larvae. These larvae then develop into pupae and settle inside a cocoon. Now they're waiting for a host so that they can start their bloodsucking. When something warm like a cat or dog appears, the pupae unzip their cocoon, jump on the animal and start feeding off it.

It was the flea that was responsible for transmitting the bubonic plague (or Black Death) that devastated Europe in the 14th century, killing tens of millions of people. It wouldn't have been much consolation for them to know that the bacterium that causes bubonic plague also kills the flea that transmits it.

But flies and fleas are amateurs compared to the mosquito, which is the creature currently responsible for the most human deaths worldwide. According to the World Health Organization, more than two million people a year die from encephalitis, the West Nile virus, dengue fever and, worst of all (in terms of numbers), malaria transmitted by these wretched insects.

It happens like this. A non-infected mosquito bites an infected person and sucks up parasites from their blood. The mosquito is then infected with the malaria parasites. The parasites go through several stages of growth inside the blood-bloated mosquito. When the mosquito then bites someone else, that person will become infected with malaria parasites, and the cycle will begin again. There is no way of telling whether a mosquito is carrying malaria or not, and at the moment there is no effective antidote to malaria. There are drugs that will stop you catching it in the first place but, alas, malaria strikes mainly in Africa and Asia, where poverty is so widespread that people can't afford these life-saving drugs that confuse mosquitoes' chemical receptors.

For make no mistake, we are dealing here with a deadly creature armed with a battery of receptors and sensors – chemical, visual and heat-seeking.

Mosquitoes can sense carbon dioxide and lactic acid – which mammals and birds give off as part of their normal breathing – from up to 35 metres away.

They have excellent visual sensors that enable them to spot anything that is moving. Mosquitoes take the view that something that moves is likely to be an excellent source of blood, so they home in on movement.

If you find yourself in malaria territory, camouflage yourself well. In particular, don't wear blue as it's been shown that mosquitoes are attracted to it more than they are to any other colour.

But that's unlikely to be enough as they also have well-developed heat sensors, so they can locate warm-blooded animals, birds and, yes, people once they get close enough.

Mosquitoes prefer children to adults, and blondes to brunettes. Certain chemicals in sweat also seem to attract mosquitoes (people who don't sweat much don't get nearly as many mosquito bites).

You're also more likely to be a target for mosquitoes if you consume bananas. However, they don't like vitamin B (as found, for example, in Marmite). So, if you're travelling to somewhere in the world where there's malaria and, for some inexplicable reason, you aren't taking anti-malarial drugs, you should grow up, darken your hair, wear an anti-perspirant, avoid sweet foods and develop a taste for Marmite on toast.

Oh, and stay away from female mosquitoes as they're the ones that bite (females need the protein from blood to produce their eggs). A female mosquito can produce 150,000,000 young in one year, which is at least 150,000,000 too many. Please don't think me callous or cruel, but mosquitoes have no useful purpose and the world would be a far better place without them.

My own personal solution is to stay away from malaria hotspots as anti-malarial drugs have potential side effects, and there are enough places in the world to visit without having to take drugs or have vaccinations. By the way, the mosquitoes that suck your blood in holiday spots up and down the Mediterranean coast do NOT carry malaria, although they can still transmit unpleasant (though not life-threatening) diseases. What a pity that I love bananas and hate Marmite . . .

The tsetse fly kills another 66,000 people annually by transmitting sleeping sickness.

The fluffy puss caterpillar looks harmless, but underneath its fluffy hair are poisonous spines. If you touch these, the spines break off and stay in your skin, causing sharp pain, then numbness, with a rash and blisters.

According to the US Department of Agriculture, the best time to spray household insects with insecticide is at four in the afternoon. Apparently, that's the time they're most vulnerable.

People used to eat woodlice – whole
and alive – thinking they were a cure for
indigestion.

Cockroaches carry germs from more than 40 different infections and diseases. These include pneumonia, typhoid fever and hepatitis.

Cockroaches – not unnaturally – also poo, and this can cause asthma and other allergic reactions in people.

Locusts can be hazardous to drivers in hot countries. If a swarm gets run over, the mess makes the roads slippery and causes traffic accidents. I think this fact is a strong candidate for the 'Oh That's Too Gross' section at the end of the book!

The banana spider from Central and South America produces enough venom to kill six adults. They have been known to turn up in bananas exported to other countries.

The Australian funnel-web spider is particularly dangerous to people – while they're sitting on the dunny (outside toilet) where these spiders like to hang out. They get their name from the tightly woven funnel-shaped webs, where they lurk in the hole at the bottom.

As regular readers will know, I don't go a bundle on wasps (Editor's translation: the author doesn't like wasps). Indeed, I posed the question *Why Wasps?* (Editor: Sorry to correct you, Mitch – actually it was: *Wasps. Why?*). Yes, to be sure, I discovered that they 'serve a useful function as predators of flies and other insects' and therefore can be used instead of pesticides but, having been stung more than once, I am not convinced.

In fact, I could quite happily live without wasps. They, on the other hand, would find it extremely difficult to live without us as they like to nest around human habitation where they can scavenge food and (sweet) liquids. This is why, on the one day a year when the weather's nice enough for a picnic, you can guarantee that large numbers of (uninvited) wasps will show up too.

If a wasp comes near you, don't flap around and scream (like I always do) because this often provokes an attack. Instead, slowly raise your arms to protect your face and stand still or move slowly away to escape. Getting stung might not be the end of it as wasp venom contains a chemical 'alarm pheromone', which, when released into the air, acts as a signal to other wasps to come and join in the stinging.

The bottom line on wasps is that although they're horrible and nasty and their sting is painful, they don't sting for the fun of it, but because they feel threatened. Also, unlike flies, fleas and mosquitoes, they are not responsible for the spread of disease.

When I was a child – many, many (*many, –* Ed.) years ago – my father's last words to me before I went to sleep were usually: 'Sleep tight and don't let the bedbugs bite.' It never occurred to me that there might be anything in it, but it turns out that not letting the bedbugs bite is an important message to heed – especially as the population of bedbugs has tripled in our major cities in recent years.

Measuring up to five millimetres in length, bedbugs feed on us, and they can consume four times their own body weight in blood in just 15 minutes.

According to a pest controller, 'Bedbugs are really on the increase and they're very hard to get rid of. They gather round the seams of mattresses and in curtains, they can hide in crevices in the bed, in cracks in the skirting board and in light fittings, and although they usually feed every five to 10 days, they can lie dormant for up to a year without feeding on a host.

'When we treat a hotel room, we don't just treat the affected room itself, but two each side of it, and the rooms immediately above and below. A female can lay up to 500 eggs in eight weeks, so if you inadvertently pick up three or four from a seat on the bus or train, you can have an infestation of thousands within two months.

'Most people call us in because they've been bitten. A bedbug will crawl onto you, pierce your skin and drink your blood through two hollow tubes. They often leave a line of bites. They don't transmit diseases, they're just pretty disgusting.

'Blood spotting on sheets or brown poo smears from the bugs are a giveaway, but people can sometimes confuse these with flea bites and they dismiss them, or they only treat the mattress, not the whole bed and bedroom, which is storing up trouble for later.

'I've seen sheets literally moving with the sheer number of bedbugs under them. In that situation you really need to take drastic action.

'Hotels are still the place where you're most likely to pick up a bedbug, because you simply don't know who has slept there before you.'

Bedbugs are thriving because we travel so much more than we used to – in Britain and abroad. So when we come back from a stay in a hotel, the bedbugs come with us. They hide in the seams of our clothes or they bury themselves in our suitcases until we get home, go to our bedrooms, take off those clothes and unpack those suitcases . . . and then out they come.

They also love the mild British climate, and can easily move from house to house. In other words, if your neighbour has them, the chances are they'll find their way over to your home. They'll even go through the cracks in the wall!

As if bedbugs aren't enough to contend with, there are also dust mites. These love mattresses – a typical mattress houses between two and three million dust mites – as well as carpets, curtains and sofas. Dust mites don't bite, but their droppings are full of allergens (things that give people allergies). When inhaled, these allergens can provoke asthma, eczema and rhinitis. In fact, house dust mites and their droppings are the most common cause of asthma worldwide.

Here's some clever camouflage. Adult head lice take on a colour to blend in with that of the person's hair in which they 'live'.

You'll read an awful lot in this book about how grisly and gruesome spiders are, so let's just put in a word for the eight-legged critters. A spider's web is a natural clotting agent. If applied to a cut, it helps stop the flow of blood. This might not tip the balance in their favour as far as you're concerned, but it's a reasonable plea in their defence.

Giant ants can be used in medicine too. Some South American tribes use them to stitch wounds. They are held next to the wound, and when they bite across it with their jaws, the 'doctor' decapitates them so the jaws are left embedded in the skin, holding the wound together.

While we're on the subject of useful creepy-crawlies . . . during the building of the Panama Canal a doctor performed an emergency operation using the light given off by a large luminous click beetle because all other sources of light had failed.

OH THAT'S TOO GROSS!

There are some species of spiders whose newly born young eat the mother's legs. It takes them quite a few weeks to finish chomping away on Mum's legs – by which time they're old enough/big enough to go and find some real prey. You might wonder why spider mothers allow their offspring to do this. Scientists think they sacrifice their legs to stop their children from eating each other. If there is such a thing as reincarnation (being born again as a different person or creature after your death) – and I, for one, don't believe there is – then you definitely wouldn't want to come back as this spider!

I wouldn't want to come back as a (male) firefly either. The female firefly attracts males by flashing her light at them. When the males turn up – presumably thinking that a night of romance lies ahead (when will they learn?) – the females eat them.

But that's nothing. As we've seen elsewhere in this book, there are female creepy-crawlies who kill their husbands after mating. The female praying mantis goes one better (or, if you stop to think about it, worse): she kills her partner *before* mating. Without going into too many of the gory details, the male praying mantis can't mate while its head is attached to its body. So, in order to mate, the female rips the male's head off.

If you put a drop of alcohol on a scorpion, it will go mad and sting itself to death.

The pinworm lays its eggs in people's bottoms. So far so bad, but you have to know why it does this: it relies on people scratching their bottoms and then putting their fingers in their mouth – thus transferring the baby pinworms to their body where they can grow. If ever there were an argument for either a) not scratching your bum, or b) washing your hands afterwards, then surely this is it.

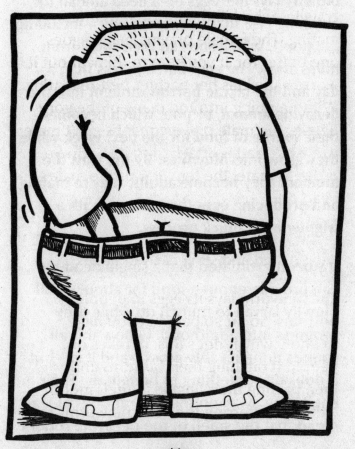

All species of fly spend some – or most – of their time in poo and other ghastly stuff, but the blowfly actually breeds in carrion and other decaying animal matter. The female blowfly lays her eggs on a dead animal (or anything else that's decomposing – including . . . poo!), which she can then smell from miles away. The eggs hatch in less than a day and the larvae burrow straight into the decaying animal, or poo, which becomes their source of food for the next week while they grow into blowflies. By the way, the moment they become adults, they're mating and producing eggs themselves so it's a frighteningly quick process.

It's been estimated that a single dead rat can provide enough food for about 4,000 blowfly larvae to munch on while they progress into adulthood. I know this all sounds unbelievably gross – and it is – but it does do something to benefit us. Their chomping away on the late rat does at least mean that the smell of the decaying rodent is removed from our delicate noses.

But that's not much of a consolation for mankind because, like other flies, the blowfly carries lots of horrid diseases from the decaying animals and poo where it spends its life, and shares them with us by vomiting on our food – or, worse, if it's given time, breeding on it. Does it come any grosser than this?

Er, yes it does! You might not have thought so, but there are worse things than death. Oh yes there are (When did this become a pantomime? Ed.). I'm talking about if you're an insect and a wasp decides that you're just the right host(ess) for her babies. Let me explain. The female wasp injects her eggs into the body of another insect (it might be a caterpillar or a spider, or any other unlucky creature that finds itself in the wrong place at the wrong time). To make sure the caterpillar (or whichever invertebrate she's chosen) doesn't reject the eggs, she also injects a chemical that interrupts the creature's immune system – effectively causing a state of stupor. The caterpillar finds itself literally rooted to the spot, unable to move. Now comes the truly ghastly bit. When the wasp's eggs are ready, they eat the caterpillar alive and work their way out through it's skin, which is then turned into an empty husk.

However, there is a good aspect to the way

that wasps 'use' caterpillars (though not as far as the caterpillars are concerned). Without these wasps, the caterpillars would end up eating a lot more of our vegetable crops.

Woodlice suffer from attacks like the ones made by wasps on caterpillars too. In their case, though, it's not from wasps, but from other insects – like, for example, the blowfly. There's also a slight difference in the method (but very little in the outcome). What happens is that the female blowfly detects a woodlouse using her brilliant sense of smell and lays her eggs in its damp home. So it's not inside the woodlouse, but in its home. Now you might think this a whole lot preferable to the scenario with the wasp and the caterpillar, but wait! The maggots that hatch from the eggs will bore their way into the woodlouse (and its family) and remain there, feeding on the tissue of their host(s). There's usually just one maggot to every woodlouse, and by the time the maggot is fully grown, the woodlouse will be nothing more than an empty shell.

All of which brings us to the botfly, which is an incredibly cunning little critter – and not an insect you want to meet if you're a mosquito. The female botfly waits until it's dark and captures a female mosquito. She then glues her eggs onto the mosquito and lets the mosquito fly off. It's not the mosquito that will hatch the eggs, but the mosquito's next victim! When the mosquito bites this victim (an animal or, I suppose, a person), the victim's body heat triggers an egg to hatch. This falls off the mosquito and burrows its way into the flesh of the new host. The larva (for that's what it is by now) secures itself with two 'hooks' and secretes a sort of antibiotic to defeat any competing bacteria and fungi. Eventually, it will emerge from the hole it makes for itself and become a grown-up botfly.

If the female botfly can't find an obliging

mosquito to deposit her eggs, she'll take whatever she can find. For example, she'll climb into the nose of an animal to lay her eggs. The resulting larvae will then feed off the poor animal's nose and mouth.

Some ribbon worms will eat bits of themselves if they can't find any food.

I know it's hard to feel pity for insects (unless they're in a Disney or Pixar film), but spare a thought for those insects that fall victim to something known as green muscardine disease (so called because of the green colour of the spores of the fungus). When these fungal spores come into contact with the body of an insect host, they penetrate it through the cuticle (the hard outer shell) and the fungus that then develops inside the body will eventually kill the insect after a few days by rotting it from the inside. Not a fun way to go – even for an insect.

People used to use cockroaches in medicine! If you were alive 2,000 years ago and you had an earache, for example, you might very well have been given ground-up cockroaches in oil.

Personally, I'd rather suffer in silence . . .

A Japanese woman had more than 50 worms removed from her stomach.

It is estimated it would take 1,120,000 mosquito bites to drain all the blood from an adult human being.

The assassin bug consumes other insects by dissolving them then sucking them up. Sometimes they dissolve and suck up one another.

If you had lived 100 million years ago, you might have met an Arthropleura. This monster relative of insects was bigger than a large man – 1.8 metres long – and it lived on the floor of the forest.

Amazon ants can do nothing except fight, so they steal the larvae of other ants and then keep them as slaves.

When a skipper caterpillar spots a wasp, it immediately shoots out loads of poo – because it knows the wasps prefer the taste of its poo – and it can make a quick escape while the wasp is dining – yum yum.

Fleas can suck blood continuously for four hours. However, their stomachs can't hold all that blood so they poo out what they can't hold and – incredibly gross fact alert – their offspring gobble up the leftovers.

I've told you about some species of baby spider feasting on their mothers' legs – like you do – but even in species where that doesn't happen, the children will still eat their mums when they die.

But gross things even up in the world of creepy-crawlies. A hungry female scorpion will sometimes eat her own offspring.

Meanwhile, the larvae of many species of horsefly will eat each other if there are no other sources of food.

The giant African snail grows to 30 centimetres long and can weigh more than 500 grams – which is heavier than the world's smallest dog.

The American authorities allow an average of 30 or more insect fragments for every 100 grams of peanut butter. To be fair to them – and to the people who eat the stuff – my guess is that the insect fragments are totally invisible to the naked eye. It's important to remember – here and elsewhere in the book – that when we talk about 'insects' and 'bugs', some of them are so microscopically small as to be totally insignificant.

In Brazil there's a species of cockroach that eats the eyelashes of young children while they're asleep.

Hookworms are parasitic worms that live in the small intestines of mammals – including, unfortunately, us. Once they get there, they suck blood from the walls of the intestines. It's reckoned that more than a billion people worldwide have them, and that they collectively lose 10 million litres of blood to these ghastly creatures every day

A 13-year-old boy in India produced winged beetles in his urine after hatching the eggs in his body.

Turn over to see a
sneak peek from another

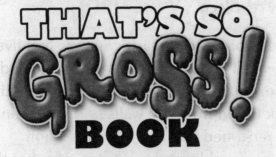

THAT'S SO
GROSS!
BOOK

ANIMALS

also look out for:

HISTORY
and
HUMAN BODY

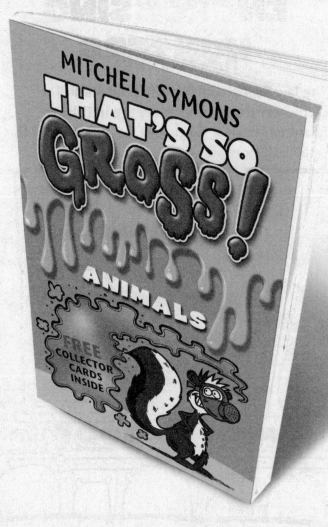

ENGROSSING HUNTERS

The law of the wild is simple but stark. The carnivores (meat eaters) eat the herbivores (plant eaters); the large and fast animals eat the small and slow animals.

ENGROSSING
FIGHTING

When they get cross, monkeys fling their poo at each other.

When tree snakes fight, they try to swallow one another.

The hyena's jaw is so powerful that it can crush bone in just a single bite.

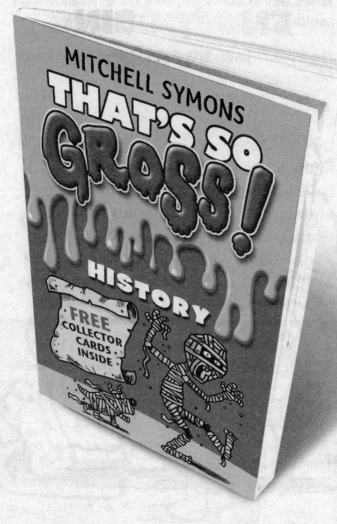

ENGROSSING LIVING

Be glad that you weren't a child in England in the Middle Ages, for if you were, you'd have been sewn into your clothes for the entire winter. This was because it was never warm enough to take them off – even in bed – and, of course, there was no central heating! The clothes would only be taken off in the spring.

Gerolamo Cardano was an Italian astrologer who predicted that he would die in 1576. Just to make sure his prediction would be right . . . he killed himself that very year. Gerolamo wasn't the only colourful character in the Cardano family. His eldest

HERE LIES
GEROLAMO
CARDANO
1501-1576

"SEE,
I TOLD YOU
I WAS ILL"

(and favourite) son was executed after murdering his wife, and another son was a gambler, who stole money from him. How did he punish him? It is said that he cut off the boy's ears.

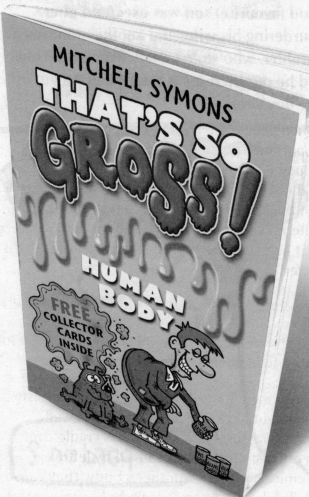

ENGROSSING BODILY FUNCTIONS

When people are trying to emphasize the importance of family over friends, they'll say: 'Blood is thicker than water.' But is it? Well, yes and no! Blood is thicker than fresh water, but is not thicker than sea water. In fact it's said that, in terms of chemical composition, the substance that human blood resembles most closely is sea water.

Fingernails grow four times faster than toenails.

Because of their elasticity, human lungs are a lot easier to blow up than a balloon.

If you've got a newborn baby brother or sister, you might have noticed flakes of . . . well, *something* on their scalp. This is cradle cap, an encrustation, that is caused by leftover chemicals from the mother's body. They cause oil glands in the baby's scalp to become active after birth.

Polydactyly is the condition where a person has more than five fingers on a hand or five toes on a foot. Where they have precisely six instead, the condition is also known as hexadactyly. Legend has it that Anne Boleyn, Henry VIII's second wife, suffered from this disorder on one hand, but an 1857 exhumation of her body disproved it. However, the actress Gemma Arterton was born with six fingers on each hand – as was the legendary West Indian cricketer, Sir Garfield Sobers. Both of them had those extra fingers removed.

Kidney stones are formed when dissolved salts in urine in the kidneys crystallize into a solid lump. I can tell you – from bitter experience – that the pain caused by these stones is absolutely excruciating. The largest known kidney stone apparently weighed 1.36 kilograms!

Leontiasis – or lion face – is a rare condition in which the facial and cranial bones in the skull overgrow. This can lead to total blindness due to compression of the optic nerve.

The letters 's', 'p' and 't' – all the consonants in the word 'spit' – produce the sounds most likely

to cause someone to spit when saying them and therefore pass on viruses, like colds and flu.

We need sleep as much as we need food – in fact more so! If you took two people and deprived one of food and the other of sleep, the one deprived of sleep would die sooner.

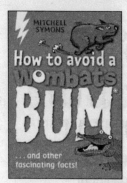

Mitchell Symons
HOW TO AVOID A WOMBAT'S BUM*
And other fascinating facts!

* Don't chase it! Wombats can run up to 25 miles per hour and stop dead in half a stride. They kill their predators this way – the predator runs into the wombat's bumbone and smashes its face.

Amaze and intrigue your friends and family with more fantastic facts and figures:

- most dinosaurs were no bigger than chickens
- Everton was the first British football club to introduce a stripe down the side of players' shorts
- A snail has about 25,000 teeth
- No piece of paper can be folded in half more than seven times

Just opening this book will have you hooked for hours!

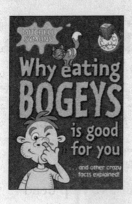

Mitchell Symons
WHY EATING BOGEYS IS GOOD FOR YOU

And other crazy facts explained!

Ever wondered . . .

- Why we have tonsils?
- Is there any cream in cream crackers?
- What's the best way to cure hiccups?
- And if kangaroos keep their babies in their pouches, what happens to all the poo?

Mitchell Symons answers all these wacky questions and plenty more in a wonderfully addictive book that will have you hooked for hours!

(And eating bogeys is good for you . . . but only your own!)

Selected for the Booktrust Booked Up! Initiative in 2008.

Q: Who writes the best books on farts, bogeys and other yucky stuff?

A: Mitchell Symons, of course

Q: What's his website called?

A: Grossbooks.co.uk, what else!

On this site you can:
- Win cool stuff in quizzes and competitions
- Add your own fab facts and publish them online
- Be first to find out about Mitchell's new books before they're published

As Mitchell's mum would say:
'Thank goodness it's not *scratch 'n' sniff...*'

See for yourself at **Grossbooks.co.uk**